The Tramp on the Lamp

A Christmas Tradition
for Adults

By
Dr. Sir Reed Lopez Windsor II

Recommended Ages: 180 months – 81 years

Though inspired by people and scenarios observed while strolling in any mall, this is a work of fiction. Names, characters, places and incidents are the products of the author's imagination, and any farfetched similarities would be a wild coincidence.

Published by Harrow McFarland LLC

ISBN-13: 978-0692462591 (Harrow McFarland LLC)
ISBN-10: 0692462597

PRINTED IN THE UNITED STATES OF AMERICA

The Legend of Kandi "Cane"

-a cautionary tale-

as told to

Dr. Sir Reed Lopez Windsor II

The Tramp on the Lamp
wasn't always a tramp.

And by no means is she some
whore in a drawer, nor a bore.

There's so much more to her lore,
from many years before...

Page 1 !

Kandi once had it all!
Her name was known
At every (good) mall.

But the kind of girl
who gives ladies a bad name.
It was about the things she had
like life was a game.

Kandi's life was full of joy...
'Til her husband walked in on the pool boy.

Kandi's ass was tossed
into the street.

No thanks to a prenup,
She was as broke as she was sweet.

Kandi's certainly no savior,
so she returns to save us
from the same behavior.

Though not logical or tragic
-maybe its holiday magic-
instead of beautiful in a mall,
she appears as a skanky discarded doll

So for this reason
where might she hide this season?

Paducah, Ky

She may spy from a cooler of wine.
One fun way to keep you in line.

She may hide
behind a door,

in a hamper,*
or on the floor.

Decatur, Ga.

*Don't smoke in a hamper!

Perhaps a good spot...
But one errant flush,
you'll need a plumber in a rush!

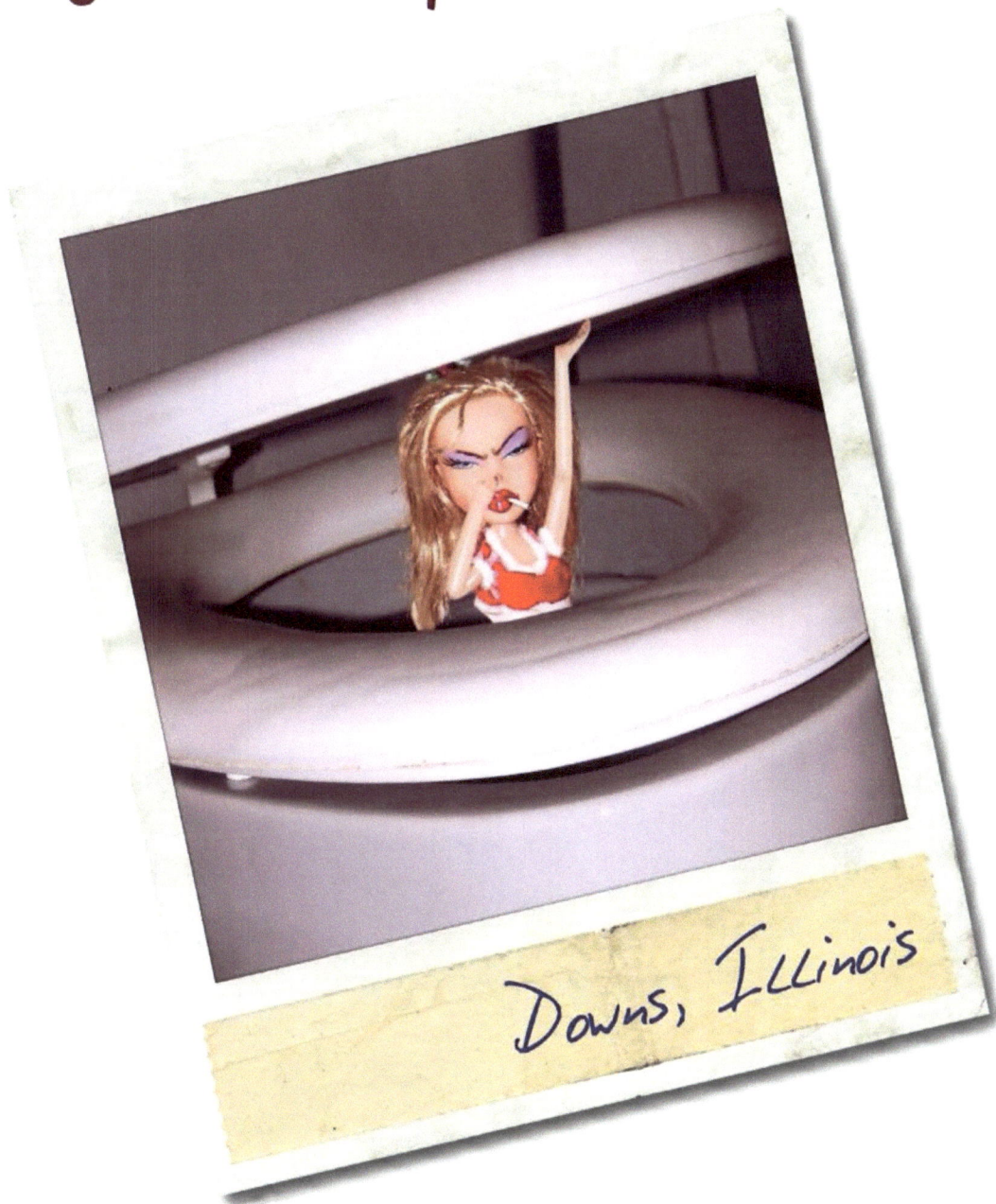

Downs, Illinois

Maybe the Tramp will be on a lamp.

Maybe a sunlamp seeking a tan.
Or a desk lamp hooking a man.

Perhaps gazing from a chandelier.
Though heights she may fear.

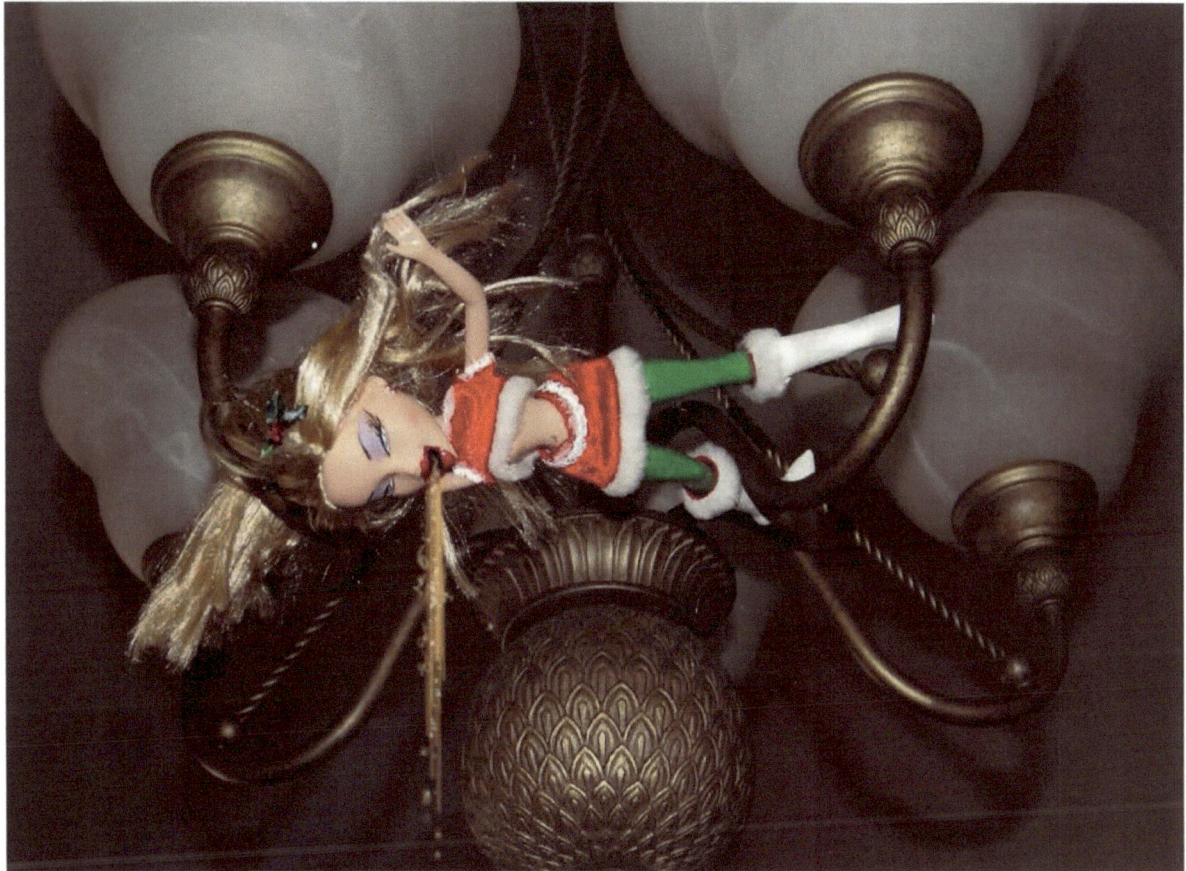

(Her stomach may be sour
from that pitiful
cougar-elf happy hour.)

Once, the Tramp hid behind a menorah during the high holiday.

After too much Manischewitz she didn't realize people could see her anyway.

Why don't these books come with Kandi dolls?
Thanks to archaic child-labor laws.

The publisher already had them on display.
But the North Korean unions took them away.

There is a moral to this whole story.

Kandi's no tramp just to be "whorey."

The Tramp hides to keep loved ones together.

To spy on us all, despite plights in any weather.

So don't ever cheat! But if you choose to anyway,

don't ever, EVER, do it during a holiday!

But if you have a moment of weakness
with such a hideous flaw,
the Tramp on the Lamp will reveal all that she saw
to Barry Cuda, Divorce Attorney at Law.

(Between you and me,
I'm sure she gets a small finder's fee.)

So as the Tramp hid
we heard all the chants,
"Happy Holidays to all, and to all,
keep it in your pants!"

The End...

Time for Holiday Activities!

Ever at a loss for words for your holiday cards?
Just cut and paste these to any Eckerd postcard!

Dearest _____,

In response to your family's holiday photo card, I don't give a mistletoe's cr*p about what countries you visited this year. I could've made the same card by going to Epcot in a day. And you should consider changing your son's name to something that won't get his nuts snapped between his cello and equestrian lessons.

I think you cry when you're alone.

Kisses XOXO,

__(Sign Here)_____

My Dear Friend _____,

We received your *adorable* family letter. I'm not trained to psychoanalyze your need to drone on about Blain's exciting promotion. I won't stoop to remind you that all children get f*cking trophies this day and age. Ashton and Madison are truly two in a million. It has nothing to do with their separate (undocumented) nannies. I assure you your letter's in a prominent spot on our refrigerator. That being said, please text us at least twenty minutes in advance of any visits.

Hugs and air kisses!!!!!!!!!!!!!!!!!!

__(Sign Here)_____

Play the

BLACK FRIDAY SURVIVAL GAME!

Who likes to save on holiday shopping? While their loved ones peacefully sleep til 10:00 a.m., burdened with having to get the same sales online?

How do you fare? Just roll a *die* (Kandi: that means one dice) to discover your fortune!

If you roll a:

1: You physically beat a Tanzanian mother in front of her baby's stroller to grab the last of two "Acme" brand console televisions.

2: You attain stardom on a viral video from a crowd scene watching a door greeter getting trampled by a street gang of obese nine-year-olds.

3: While looking your absolute worst, in a stained t-shirt and in a crazed mental state, you run into everyone you ever dated in high school.

4: You wonder, quite simply, what our world has come to. Then you help a clerk give birth in the NASCAR aisle, renewing your faith in mankind.

5: You get the genius idea that the term "Black Friday" is racist and you file a massive class-action lawsuit. You're ultimately awarded $10,000,000 in emotional damage and then overjoyed to watch Miley Cyrus portray your plight onscreen.

6: You decide to sleep-in at home, enjoy your day, and buy everything on Black Monday from the comfort of your work computer.

No-Joy Thin Mints

- Dried toothpaste (from your sink)
- Chocolate-style flavored syrup
- Razor blade

Are you dreading making a dessert for a holiday party that you're not thrilled about attending? Take a razor blade that's lying around and chisel off the dried toothpaste from your sink into appealing patties.

Drizzle with chocolate syrup and the magic begins. Cheap green toothpaste looks festive with brownish syrup. Tell the kids Santa's elves eat them or it makes deer fly or whatever. Yay.

Pixie Dust

Ingredients:
- Candy canes
- Hammer

Go out outside of your trailer or carport to a hard, flat surface and smash the candy canes with all the rage you can muster. Scrape all the shards and powder together and there you have your pixie dust.

Use the dust to:
- Make things that go in your mouth taste more tolerable.
- Suppress the gag reflex.
- Blow in the eyes of potential attackers.
- Sell in Ziplocs prior to quick exits.

Enjoy.

Fun *New* Uses for Fruit Cake

Have you re-received another fruit cake?

1. Use as a Duraflame log. Mystery fruit makes calming fumes.

2. Makes a great doorstop, rated up to Category-1 hurricane winds.

3. Placed near a mound, one cake will kill most varieties of Mexican fire ants.

4. Use as a "pen cushion" for pens and pencils.

5. Use it to keep a car or small Cessna from rolling down any incline.

6. Duct tape it to any troublesome corpse you're trying to submerge.

7. Let it absorb a bottle of rum and rename it "Caribbean rum cake" or some other nonsense. Kids will sleep like a coma patient on cold medicine.

8. Navy Seal fun fact: If a fruitcake strikes the correct point on the cranium, the target will be knocked unconscious without any telltale bruise.

9. Put chunks of it in your enemy's pockets and they'll get seized by airport security in those sniffer machines for terrorist activity.

10. Just save it and re-gift it next year. Or the next.

For those of you with no patience for nonsense here are some *real* recipes

Holiday Cocktails –Yay!

"I find that cocktails help lubricate any important decision-making decisions."

–Kandi

The Kandi Kane

1 shot vanilla rum
1 shot white chocolate liqueur
1 shot peppermint Schnapps
Candy cane for garnish

Add all liquids to a cocktail shaker filled with ice. Shake well and strain into a martini glass. Garnish with a candy cane. Takes like three seconds and makes those around you seem 1% more interesting.

Kandi Kane Christmas Mojito

For Infusion:
2 cups mint leaves
1 bottle of vodka, Albertson's, no one will know
For cocktail:
1 tbs. crushed candy canes
1 1/2 oz. mint-infused vodka (above)
1/2 oz. B&B (Benedictine and brandy)
1/2 oz. half-and-half
Peppermint stick
Mint sprig (garnish)

For Infusion:
Place mint leaves into a pitcher. Empty vodka into the container and muddle slightly. Store in a cool place for at least 3 days - longer for a stronger taste.

For cocktail:
Place crushed candy into a pint glass. Muddle the candy slightly, don't over-muddle into a dust. Add vodka, brandy and half-and-half and stir. Pour into a shaker with ice. Shake lightly to chill and strain into an old-fashioned glass of ice. Add a peppermint stick and stir. Garnish with a mint sprig. Amaze your friends or make new ones with more money.

Puerto Rican Rum & Coconut Milk Christmas Cocktail
Six of my favorite things in one title? It's true.

1 can (15-ounce) coconut milk
1 can (14-ounce) condensed milk
1 can (12-ounce) evaporated milk
1 cup Puerto Rican white rum
2 egg yolks
Pinch of salt
1/4 teaspoon ground cinnamon

Place all ingredients in a blender and process for 3 minutes on high until foamy. Store in a chilled glass pitcher in the refrigerator and serve cold, sprinkled with the cinnamon.

Easy to have as your straggler friends come stumbling in like hobos at all hours.

Slow-Cooker Cocktails? Can This Be True?

Fun fact: 92% of all trailer counters already hold slow cookers. Imagine cocktails already brewing away, awaiting your return after a hard day's work at the DMV. This isn't another too-good-to-be-true meth-induced dream.

Here are two recipes for slow-cooker holiday cocktails.

Slow-Cooker Peppermint Hot Cocoa

Whisk six 12-ounce cans of evaporated milk (don't bitch about quantity, it's the holidays, Walmart, dollar store…) 1/3 cup chocolate liqueur and 1/4 cup peppermint schnapps in a crock pot. Mix in two 12-ounce bags of any dark chocolate chips. Cover and cook on low heat for 2 to 3 hours, stirring occasionally.

Proceed to your fulfilling jobs. Come home and ladle into mugs. Garnish with whipped topping and candy canes, sit back in your corduroy beanbag chairs, watch reruns of Hee Haw and thank me later.

Crock o' Christmas Chai

Pour 8 cups of boiling water into your slow cooker. Add 16 chai tea bags. Close the lid tight and let the bags steep for about 10 minutes. Remove the tea bags and then stir in 1/2 cup each of spiced rum and vanilla-flavored vodka and 2 cinnamon sticks. Cover and cook on low for about 2 hours. Stir in 2 cups sweetened condensed milk; switch to the warm setting until ready to serve. Ladle into mugs and garnish with cinnamon sticks. I have nothing witty to add because there's nothing funny about this magical formula that's either from the Orient, the North Pole or Kentucky.

Mexi-Cocoa! - Cocoa with a BITE
Drink anytime without looking like an alcoholic

- 1 tbs. unsweetened cocoa powder
- 1 tsp. cinnamon
- Dash of cayenne pepper
- Dash of chili powder
- 3/4 cup almond milk (Vegans finally get their day, or Irish cream, or milk, yada, yada)
- Splash of agave nectar (or honey or maple syrup…)
- 1 oz. Silver tequila
- Paprika
- Peppermint stick to garnish for your trite Facebook update

In a saucepan on low add the cocoa, cinnamon, chili powder and cayenne. Toast until the spices release their buzz-worthy aromas, within minutes. Using a whisk, slowly swirl-in the milk. Raise the temp to medium and bring to a simmer. Stir in the agave nectar and remove from the heat. Rim a mug by dipping into a saucer of water and blotting into a dish of paprika. Pour in tequila. Add hot cocoa mixture. Stir with a peppermint stick and serve. How's that for a Facebook update! The envy of your miserable "friends."

LETTERS TO THE EDITOR

Dear Editor,

I am fuming! In your "fable's" mere 422 words you've managed to be misogynistic, with clumsy jabs at the blonde stereotype and vilifying *entire* industries of attorneys, plastic surgeons and pool maintenance workers. This book has left me with searing abdominal cramps, thus *ruining* another holiday season. BRAVO (sarcasm intended!)

Mrs. Cookie Hollingsworth, Rockdale Estates, Connecticut

Dear Mrs. Hollingsworth,

You counted the words? What were you thinking when you saw the cover? Even if you read the title in braille! We endeavored to equally poke fun at as many things as possible within our "mere 422 words." We'll pray for you.

Dear Editor,

In, like, some pictures the tramp looks human even though her head and eyes are too big. Then she's a pixie or elf or whatever. Did I miss how she transforms? Was it Christmas magic or something? Or maybe there's a page missing?

Travis Lee Ray, c/o American Van Stand, Epps, Arkansas.

Dear Mr. Lee Ray,

Dude, it's a f*ckin humor book! Christ, read the title. I mean, Rudolph was about a flying deer, man. Frosty was made of frozen water!

Question: Is "Kandi Cane" the Tramp on the Lamp's real name?

Thelma-Lou Waxman from Mattoon, Illinois.

Answer: No. Kandi's birth name was Punkin O'Bromowitz, a nice Irish girl from Bowling Green, KY.

Regretfully, we're no longer able to accept you people's letters.

JOB OPPORTUNITIES

Work at **Tramp on the Lamp's** headquarters in Muncie, Indiana!
Great experience for kids home from school!

We're Seeking:

DRIVERS – For almost-gourmet food trucks serving cocktails, mistletoe hookahs and standard holiday fare at carnivals, gun shows and foreclosed strip malls. (We frown on applicants with DUI's within past two years.)

COSTUMED GREETER – Are you blonde and *"easy on the eyes?"* We'll supply the Kandi "Tramp" costume, you provide curvy attitude. To give out samples at MallMart of our new *Tramp on the Lamp* Kielbasa ™. Also for bachelor parties, bar mitzvahs and bible retreats.

BANK DEPOSITERS – We need folks with clean records to help make small cash deposits (under $9,999 USD) in banks, spread geographically 'round the region. *Discretion a must, passport a plus!*

COMPLAINT PROCESSERS – Sometimes the ol' mailbag gets bogged down with negative Nellies whining about this & that. We need some sharp-tongued Sallies who can dish it right back! Need the wisdom to know which letters to shred and which ones to pass up to the boss.

SECURITY FOLKS – To help Travis at the front gate –and should have a workable knowledge of harassment laws, defamation thresholds, "sweep" for concealed devices, human pressure points, and have a understanding of nations with no U.S. extradition policies.

HOUSEKEEPER – Mostly for the author's residence and the upkeep of the author's alleged baby boy. If you're hovering around eighteen years of age, author reserves the right to adopt you for tax benefits that don't involve you. Must have a "green card" since author still entertains fantasies of running for office one day.

Kandi Says: Our "interns" don't get paid,
but how can you put a price on experience?

Coming Soon...

The Tramp on the Lamp must thank all who came before her:

Her cousin, that feeble Shelf Elf; her niece, the Whore in a Drawer (with more daddy-dwarf issues than she); her cousin from Georgia, the Pixie from Dixie; her favorite uncle in Key West, the Fairy on a Ferry; her cousin Marislaysis, the hooker in the slow-cooker. And lastly, this book wouldn't have been possible without a loan from the Skank at the Bank.

About the Author

Dr. Sir Reed L. Windsor II, about to sneeze, circa 1971

Dr. Sir Reed Lopez Windsor II has endeavored to be a learned gentleman.

He attended finishing schools and has traveled the globe seeking tutelage and counseling after witnessing a parent committing adultery near a Christmas tree during the holidays.

Dr. Windsor hopes this book will be an important step in the healing process.